Toys, Tools, Guns & Rules

A Children's Book About Gun Safety

By Julie Golob
Illustrated by Nancy Batra

This book is dedicated to my two amazing children and my loving parents.

With gratitude:

There are so many people who have helped me on this journey–my amazing husband, who supports me on my many projects and is my immediate springboard for questions and ideas; Lois Chase, my person who can fix anything; Nancy Batra, for her illustrative talents; and Rob Staeger, for his editing brilliance and guidance. Thank you also to Gabby Franco, Barbara Baird, Kimberly Kolb Eakin, Tisma Juett, and Kirstin Bennett for their advice and helpful insight.

The saying "It takes a village" is true. My village has been an incredible support network online. To Malcom S., Dan T., and my social media community, thank you so very much for your kind words, your shares, and your valuable feedback. As I try to tell you often, you're the best!

Toys are **FUN** things you can play pretend with.

What is your favorite toy?

Do you know what a **TOOL** is?

Adults use tools to help them get a job done.

What are some of your favorite TOYS that look like tools?

Knife

Hammer

Saw

Chainsaw

Real tools
are
NOT toys.

Here are some tools
that are not toys.

A
GUN
is a tool for many grown-ups.

It is NOT a toy.

Another word for gun is firearm.

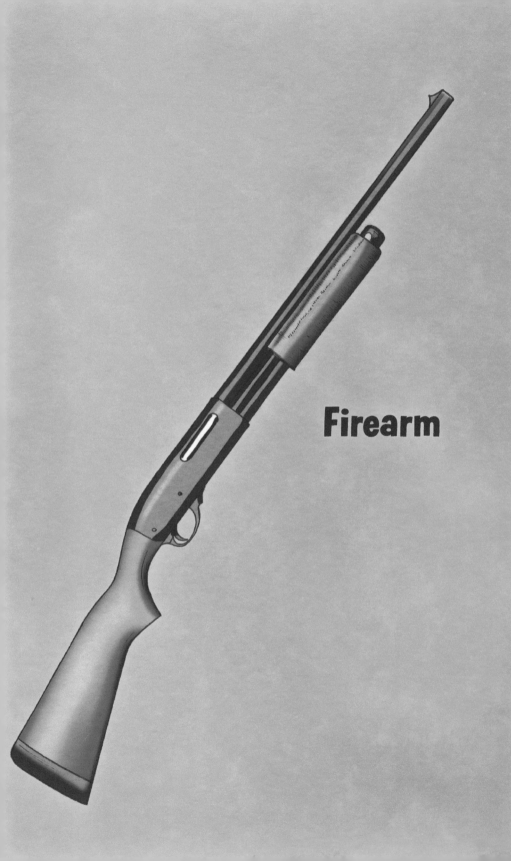

Firearm

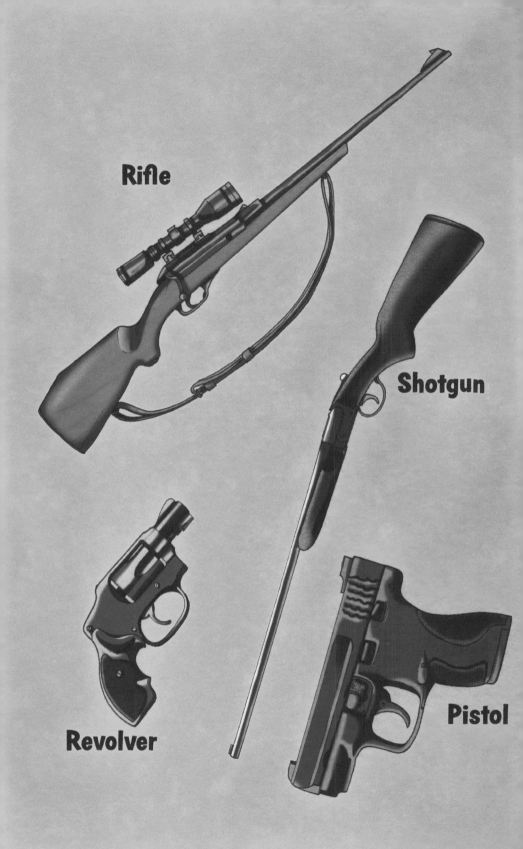

Rifle

Shotgun

Revolver

Pistol

Guns come in different shapes and sizes.

Just like you should be **CAREFUL** around **tools,** you should also be

VERY CAREFUL

around guns.

GUNS shoot **BULLETS** that fly very **FAST** through the air.

The bullets make holes in the things they hit.

Muzzle

A **BULLET** flies out of the end of the gun with the **BIG HOLE** in it.

It's called the muzzle.

This part of the
gun is called the
TRIGGER.

Pulling the trigger
is what makes a gun
SHOOT.

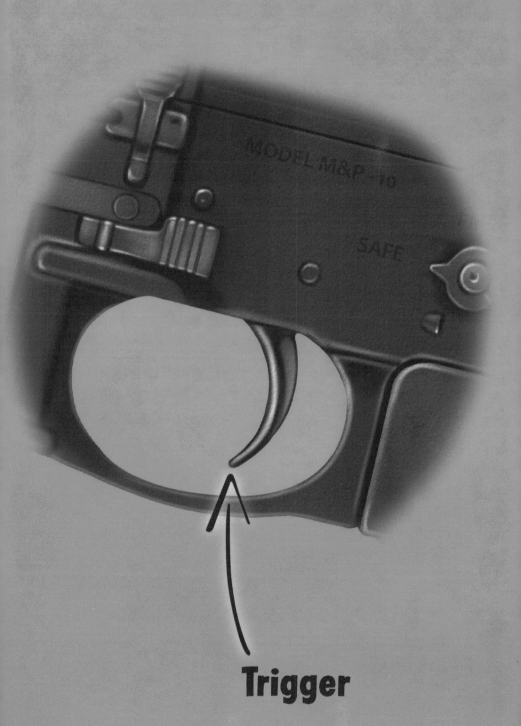

Trigger

A **GUN** is a **TOOL** for many grown-ups.

Guns can **HURT** you, but they can keep you **SAFE**, too.

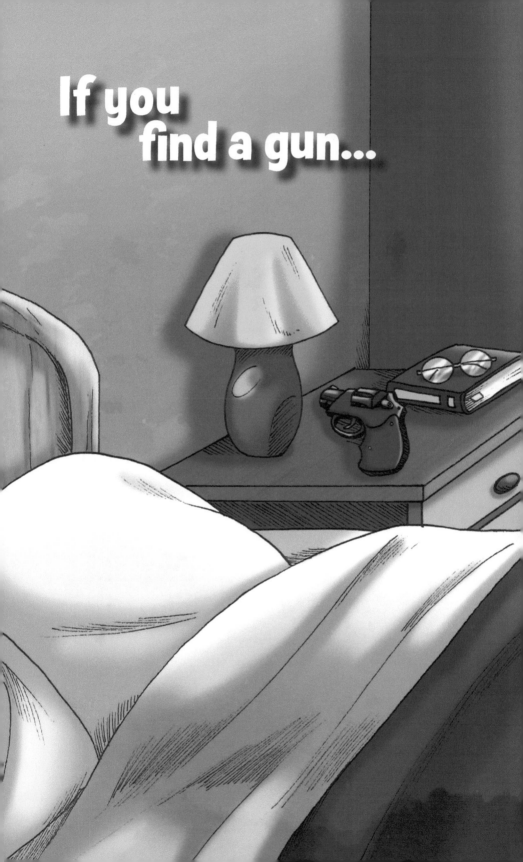

DON'T TOUCH IT!

Safe

When it comes to guns, there are **RULES.**

They should be put away in a **SAFE PLACE** when they are not being used.

Do you have questions about GUNS and other TOOLS?

Guns are a polarizing topic, and talking to children about them can be difficult. The Congressional Research Service estimates there are more than 300 million firearms in the United States. The sheer number of guns in America, combined with references to them and their usage in the media and entertainment industry, means it's time to start this important discussion with our children.

Who is this book for?

Toys, Tools, Guns & Rules is written for young children to help them learn about guns and the importance of respecting firearms.

What is the goal?

We talk to kids about strangers, fire, drugs, and the dangers of drowning, but not about guns. Regardless of which side of the gun-control debate we fall on, in order to protect our children and help prevent deaths with firearms, we need to talk to children about guns and firearm safety.

When do you start the discussion?

Education is critical, and this book is written for children as young as 3 years old. It's never too early to get started, though. *Toys, Tools, Guns & Rules* is a tool for adults to start conversations with their own children about guns as early as possible.

Where does this book apply?

Anywhere a child can learn! Whether it's in school, at home, or in a library, firearm safety should be a priority for parents and educators.

Why this book?

Author Julie Golob is a U.S. Army veteran who has completed military police training as well as being one of the most accomplished competition shooters in the world. She's also a parent of two young children, and she strongly believes that demystifying guns and learning firearm safety is critical to reducing gun violence and accidents. Read the additional resource guide and access other useful information at the end of the book.

Toys, Tools, Guns & Rules

A Parents' Guide

A Parents' Guide

We talk to kids about the dangers of fire, drugs, strangers, drowning, and more—but not about guns. Despite how polarizing the media and politics have made the topic of firearms, we must talk with our children about guns and firearm safety to protect them and help prevent deaths and injuries. As a mom of two young children, I wrote *Toys, Tools, Guns & Rules* to teach my daughters about guns and firearm safety at a young age. In this guide I will explain how I use this book and offer suggestions on how to begin the conversation about guns with kids.

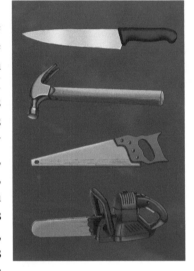

The first few pages of this book establish the differences between toys and real tools. I've included a variety of toys and adult tools in these spreads. When you read these pages, I suggest you point out different toys and tools that you have in your home. The toys and tools on these pages provide comparisons that many children will already understand. For example, you may have hammers and saws at home, and most people cook with a hot oven from time to time. You have likely established rules at home for your children about the stove, scissors, and other potentially dangerous objects. Talk about them and your home rules as you read these pages.

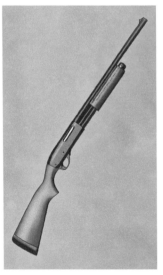

The first page with a firearm is straight and to the point. The background is purposefully yellow, a color signifying caution. The first firearm pictured is a shotgun, a very popular firearm for sporting purposes. Shotgun shooting is even an Olympic sport, and this firearm represents one commonly used in the United States and around the world for hunting, competition, and even home defense.

My goal with the next series of pages is to further demystify firearms and begin to establish rules. Children may know or have seen a variety of firearms on television, and it's important to teach that they can come in different shapes and sizes, materials, and even colors. In order to make a personal correlation to your children's lives, this is a great time to address any firearms you may own or guns that your child may be exposed to.

Now that we have addressed a variety of types of firearms, it's important to discuss how they work. In one spread I show a bullet speeding toward a target, but children should also understand that bullets can pierce through paper, plastic, wood, and even some metal. Kids may have additional questions that can be tough to answer. Do your best to answer clearly and logically, to help keep emotion and intrigue at bay.

In the next pages, we explore the anatomy of a firearm, with emphasis on two important components—the muzzle and the trigger. Learning how firearms work can help children be safe when they are around guns. Knowing that a bullet leaves the firearm's muzzle is a first step. I use these pages to tell my children that if they ever see the muzzle end of a firearm pointed at them, it's a very bad thing and that they are in danger.

The trigger is another key part of firearm anatomy that children should learn about. It's the part of the gun that is most enticing for them to touch. Beyond the universal messages of "stop" and "don't touch firearms," helping children understand why and how firearms work can help alleviate the fascination factor. These two pages are deliberately colored red to further ingrain the importance and potential danger.

Next we establish who uses firearms. This page can help your child understand

that firearms are around them every day, and that they are not only used by criminals. Firearms are tools, and are used safely and responsibly by adults they may know and encounter. Competition shooters, hunters, everyday lawful gun owners, service members, and law enforcement officers all use firearms. You may own firearms, too.

The next few pages address a common fear parents have, one in which a child finds an unsecured gun. We see a young boy knock on a bedroom door. Inside the room, a revolver is clearly visible on the nightstand. On the next spread, the boy is talking to an adult. She could be his mother, an aunt, or a care provider—she symbolizes someone the child trusts. The firearm is no longer pictured; this is intentional. Observant children will ask where it went. This represents a great moment where you can answer the question, similar to how the woman on the page is speaking with the young boy. It's also an opportunity to draw a correlation between what you see on the page and your own home and experience.

This is an excellent time to let children know that they should come to you with their questions about guns. Some questions may be difficult for you to answer, but telling children that you will always do your best to find answers and be honest will build trust and let them know that you care.

Next the book showcases safe storage. Safe firearm storage can be represented by a vault-like safe, as pictured, or smaller safes and gun locks. These pages give you the chance to share with children your personal experience with safe storage. Maybe you or a family member has a visible gun safe in the home. Adding personal stories to your reading of this book will help build trust further. Firearms should be secured safely when they are not in use to prevent theft and access.

The last scene shows a playground with a city and mountains visible in the distance. Firearm safety goes beyond small towns or country living. It's a topic that families should address no matter where they live. The final question of the book—"Do you have questions about guns and other tools?"—helps adults keep the conversation going.

The illustrations in *Toys, Tools, Guns & Rules* reflect my desire to represent a variety of ethnicities of both the adults and children in this book. This is not a location, race, or male/female issue. A firearm is an object without feelings, and cannot distinguish the color of a person's skin, their orientation, or their beliefs. I have avoided specific stereotypes in this book and all characters are fictitious, but they can represent people in real life. Firearm safety is for everyone.

Firearm Safety Rules Adapted for Children

Gun safety is serious and not something to fool around with. To be safe, follow these rules:

1. Always treat guns as if they are loaded and can shoot.

2. Never point the muzzle of a gun at anything you don't want to destroy.

3. Always keep your finger off a gun's trigger unless it is pointed at a safe target and you are ready to shoot it.

4. Bullets are powerful, so remember:
   You must know what your target is and also know what's behind it.

Resources

Visit kidsgunsafetybook.com for additional information and free resources to learn more on how to use this book and talk to children about gun safety.

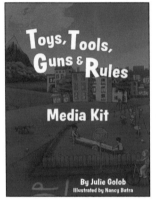  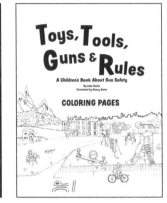

Project ChildSafe®
Project ChildSafe is a program by the National Shooting Sports Foundation to promote firearm safety and education through the distribution of educational messages, free firearm safety kits, and gun locks. Visit projectchildsafe.com to learn more about safe storage, take a firearm safety pledge, and more.

Eddie Eagle GunSafe® Program
The Eddie Eagle GunSafe program is a gun accident prevention program developed by a task force made up of educators, school administrators, curriculum specialists, urban housing safety officials, clinical psychologists, law enforcement officials, and National Rifle Association firearm safety experts. You can learn more at eddieeagle.nra.org, where you'll find downloadable materials designed for children in Pre-K through fourth grade.

About the Author

Julie Golob is a decorated multi-time world and national champion, and a U.S. Army veteran, firearms instructor, and mother. She is a prominent voice for sharing safe, responsible gun ownership throughout the firearms industry, the shooting sports, and beyond. Golob's first book, *SHOOT: Your Guide to Shooting and Competition* is a primer on improving shooting skills and how to get started in the shooting sports. She has also written a short eBook: *Shooting While Pregnant: A Resource for Expecting Moms. Toys, Tools, Guns & Rules*, which encourages families to start the conversation about guns early, is her first children's book.

Find her online at JulieGolob.com

CPSIA information can be obtained
at www.ICGtesting.com
Printed in the USA
LVHW071946070723
750629LV00012B/18